I Am My Mother's Disappointments

Copyright © 2024 Victoria Hood

All rights reserved. No part of this book may be reproduced in any form or by any electronic or mechanical means, including information storage and retrieval systems, without prior written permission of both the publisher and the copyright owner, except for the use of brief quotations in critical articles and reviews.

The events described in this book represent the recollection of the author as she experienced them.

Cover design by Matthew Barkley

ISBN 9781737380689 (hardcover)
ISBN 9781737380696 (ebook)

First Edition
Published by Girl Noise Press
girlnoise.net

Praise for Victoria Hood

"These poems are a raw, deeply personal, at times heart breaking exploration of the authors mother's death, the grieving process, eating disorders, complex mother-daughter relationships and guilt. Like reading a private diary or hearing someone's confessions, this is a beautifully written ode to family and how we love them despite their flaws which I felt honoured as a reader to be let into. I can't wait to read more of Hood's work."

— MOLLY LLEWELLYN, EDITOR OF *PEACH PIT*

"In *I Am My Mother's Disappointments*, Victoria writes, and keeps writing, showing us how loss too can change, meaning the aim is not to diagnose it — how boring — but to continue. This realism holds how not to be sad, which means to keep living: as a wife, a lover, a sister, a daughter, a person in recovery, a working writer, who wants to be.

This is not a confessional because there is no stuck guilt, and more importantly, no need to be seen to be understood. I want to eat spaghetti with this person. I want to thank her for writing about death without forgetting the body and our world: how it works now, and what it can become. It's the most hopeful text I've read in a long time."

— MAIREAD CASE, AUTHOR OF *TINY* AND *SEE YOU IN THE MORNING*

"I'm so glad Victoria forgot to get over her mother's death. I'm so glad she forgot to feel shame about her desires. I'm so glad she forgot to be nice and quiet, forgot to restrain herself, forgot to acquiesce and apologize. Instead of a quiet forgetting, *I Am My Mother's Disappointments* is a loud remembrance. It celebrates, it rages, this book makes noise — honest and fearless and messy noise, strange and wonderful and complicated noise. A must-read for anyone who has a mother or who has lost a mother or who has never had a mother. Victoria is President of the Dead Parent Club and I hope she never moves on."

— HOLLIE ADAMS, AUTHOR OF *THINGS YOU'VE INHERITED FROM YOUR MOTHER*

"Does grief ever end? Who do we become in the long wake of loss? Victoria Hood's *I Am My Mother's Disappointments* is a rare thing: an account of long grief in all its absurdity and complexity. By turns harrowing, playful, vulnerable, angry, and just plain funny, Hood's poems, flash nonfictions, and linguistic contraptions explore how death shapes our lives in incisive and ridiculous ways. A genuine and uncategorizable marvel."

— GREG HOWARD, AUTHOR OF *HOSPICE*

"Victoria Hood has written a grief book that echoes with silence. If I weighed *I Am My Mother's Disappointments* I am certain it would weigh infinity. It would shatter the scales. It weighs as much as a daughter's longing for her mother. It is that heavy. Hood has composed a beautiful, raging howl."

— SABRINA ORAH MARK, AUTHOR OF *WILD MILK*

"I have been reading Victoria's work since she was very young. I've followed her progression as a writer, a human, and a Hood. Although the family often disagrees on our facts, Victoria captures our truth in these words. She artfully bares her soul, my soul, our family's soul, beautifully."

— JUSTIN HOOD, FATHER OF VICTORIA HOOD

Also by Victoria Hood

My Haunted Home: Stories (FC2)
Death and Darlings (Bottlecap Press)
Entries of Boredom and Fear (Bottlecap Press)

I Am My Mother's Disappointments

poems by
Victoria Hood

GIRL NOISE
PRESS

for the dead parent club and the memories that keep us up at night

mom

Table of Contents

The Pact 01
Forgetful 03
A List of People Who Should Masterbate to Me 06
Is It What You Wished For? 09
The Boy of It All 14
There's Another One, Though 16
Cut 18
The Things 20
thnx for the memories 24
The Gossip 28
Learning to Forget 33
I am the killer 35
one day your mom will die too 37
past! present! 40
Warning Signs 47
You'd Be So Happy 51
But I Do Not Know About Dad 52

The Pact

I told my mother I was suicidal,
I told her I had thoughts of suicide
        I had thoughts of killing myself
        I thought thoughts about ending my life
                      my dumb life

She told me she understood
She told me we have a pact
    you go, I go
            This was her way of making me *not want to*
            This was her way of *deterring me*

And then she killed herself.
I linger behind her
            not holding up my end of the bargain

you go, I go

Not a question

you go, I go

She went and I lingered

> It is important to mention I am not ready
> For any commentary on my mother
> or on myself
> or on anything
> really

Is she still waiting for me just over the edge somewhere?
In my moments of loneliness I think of our pact
    she would have kept her end of the deal
    but *what kind of mother wants her daughter to keep that deal*
        Would my mother?
        Is she lingering too?

you go, you wait, you lonely, you dead, you body, you ashes in a room in a house, you overdosing while your kids come home from school, you go, you did it, that was easy,
I stay, I linger, I miss

Forgetful

I forgot to get over your death.

I must have thought about it a few times,
    but the thoughts always escaped me
            evaded me
            left me
                    dusting rubble from my knees

It is about time now, people tell me,
    that women grow the fuck up
It is about time now, I have been told,
    that little girls need to get it together
It is about time now, my teachers whisper,
    she writes anything not about her mother
      we are all so tired hearing about a woman we don't know
           reading about a woman we can
                    never meet
          lingering inside a dead body

VICTORIA HOOD

. . .

I forgot to get over your death,
but I do not rest flowers on your grave
                                        we were too poor for that shit
instead we put you inside a container with leaf decor,
you were always so orange and crispy,
so fragile
so breakable
so weak

I forgot to get over your death,
So I am stuck in limbo,
writing my way out of you.

family family family
if you're reading this and regretting it already,
please stay and get to know me

A List of People Who Should Masturbate to Me

※

I hope your mirror gets all junked-up
                gets all fucked-up
                gets all foggy

We'll start off easy: my husband,
but even before we were dating you told me you used to
picture me,
when we were both in high school,
I was a little scene kid who never ate,
you wack it to me now   (and I watch)

The next step: my husbands best friend,
because who doesn't want what they can't have?
who doesn't love to think about the off-limits,
think about how you can't have me, how sweet
it would be to get me

I AM MY MOTHER'S DISAPPOINTMENTS

More, more, more: any teacher I had in college,
with my *revealing* nature,
with my *naked* mind, yearning
for some sort of excitement

Please don't stop now: both of my ex-girlfriends,
the one who got religious wishing for teenage lust on the tongue,
the one who won't speak to me,
thinking of the times she did
(or maybe the times she couldn't)

Harder, harder: my friends who sit on my couch after we
almost, basically, had sex on New Years Eve,
I hope you sit there and think of me kissing you,
I hope you squirm at not being able to touch me,
I hope you spit in my mouth one day

I'm not done yet: my best friend,
who has seldom talked about her sexuality,
who lives her sexuality, with no discussion,
who I love to kiss — drunk and sloppy,
Think of me.

The years pass and I collect: my boyfriend,
always looking for pictures of me
to cast alongside the pictures he collects of other
men and women and people with any genitalia,
I will lead the army to your cock.

Just finish already: me, sometimes,
when I have no one else in mind,
when I wonder if it's possible to be turned on by myself,
when I want something fulfilling,
when I want to be fulfilled.

I hope it was as good for you, as it was for me.

Is It What You Wished For?

Look, mom, I'm sorry, or maybe you're proud, or maybe I just made it all up, but I'm eating again.

Or really, I'm eating and able to keep eating.

Sometimes I sit down and I eat and I do not think about what will attach to my bones, I do not over analyze the ways in which I need to peel apart the piece of chicken *string by string* just to be able to enjoy anything.

I don't know if you realized, but when you start eating after not eating for years you will **[gain weight]**

And that is scary when you told me for so long that *[thin is beautiful]*

But you were not thin in your death, you were thin in your youth. You were thin because you were homeless, because your parents left you, because you were starving by chance, by a lack of means.

I was thin in my youth, because my mind hates me, because I hate me, because you told me if I told you that I wouldn't eat it then I would go to bed hungry — you promised me I could be hungry.

You were always so stubborn about your rules, you could never change your mind. So I told you I liked nothing, nothing, I like to eat the air, I like the taste of hunger in my lungs, I am a fiend for desperation covered in bone dust. I am a slut for a good rib cage.

You fell in love and I remember you that way. I remember you plump with love in your heart, I remember you eating and joking and farting on each other in the kitchen. When I think of you, Mom, I think of your beautiful smile.

But if you saw me now would you notice I was happy? Or, would you wonder why your daughter had gained seventy-five pounds over the past few years?

You were always a witch, you always made things come true. So when you died and I got hungry I knew you cast a spell on me, or maybe you cursed me, I think it depends who you ask.

It was harder to starve myself after you killed yourself — I'm sure there is something poetic there, something lingering and haunting, but this is a venture into looks, it is an exploration of vanity.

It was harder to starve myself after you killed yourself, but I could still manage. It wasn't until Husband came along that things got much easier,
        that things got so much easier.

I AM MY MOTHER'S DISAPPOINTMENTS

I finally listened to Sister who told me I looked sick and dying and being fat is not a sin.

I found others to love me while I fed myself, I found others to help me love feeding myself.

I watched you in the kitchen with Dad and I loved the way he looked at you like you were everything he always wanted. Maybe me and you, Mom, just weren't meant to be skin and bones. Not after we fell in love. Mom, I'm sorry to say, but your curse worked and now I have *some meat on these bones*.

I remember overhearing you when I was younger correcting someone for telling me I was lucky to be naturally skinny, you shook your head and told them I had to work for it. I remember thinking you were such a bitch, you were just jealous, you were just old and tired. But you weren't wrong, I did have to work for it. It was hard to feel so bloated and diseased, it was hard to not want to eat, to smell smell smell and not want a single bite, it was hard. But I'm sure you felt that in another way, in your youth where you could not eat for other reasons.

Maybe I should have apologized then — I'm sorry for choosing not to eat when you had no choice. If it helps, it still haunts. I feel selfish and rude.

But you were right. Naturally, I am about as average as they come. Naturally, I am not just skin and bones. Naturally, I am just like everyone else, I am not special.

i sit in corners staring at walls trying to make you appear

it seems like whenever i am looking for you you are hiding

are you too ashamed to face me? is there something you are carrying with you that you don't want me to see? what could you possibly still be hiding, mother?

you are a woman of secrets,
you always have been,
i get to know you more every day

would we have been friends if i wasn't your child?

who would you have birthed if not me?

why am i so proud that i am like my dad?

The Boy of it All

I think you'd like him, I really think you would.

He is tall, he is nice, he laughs like a dinosaur.

I think you'd like the way he holds me together, the way he holds himself together, the way we both become limp yarn together.

I'm sorry you couldn't be at the wedding, but we saved you a seat. Front row. Next to your husband. And your best friend. (oh, did you hear the gossip, mother? stay tuned.)

I cried without you there, I cried thinking maybe you wouldn't want me to do this — not like this — but maybe I should have pushed harder to elope, I should have yelled and screamed and got my way more (I know you would have done that for me).

I think so much about how different it would be with you there. I think so much about the things you'd throw and the people you'd piss off. Mostly, I think so much about how you would have made sure it felt like my day.

Don't worry, it still did. Moreso, I guess, it felt like our day. Like me and Husband had finally conjoined into the one being we were hoping to.

Don't be mad, but we used your wedding rings. I'm sure you wouldn't be, but I like to preface. It was the first thing I called when you died, *I want Mom's wedding ring*. I knew if I got married with your rings we would stay so far in love we couldn't get up.

I was right Mom, and I think you'd love him. He is not a disappointment, it's just my lack of a backbone that is. We laugh about how uncomfortable you'd make him (which is always your favorite). We laugh at memories and he pretends to know you, I think he's getting close to almost understanding, *life isn't the same without your mommy.*

There's Another One, Though

I think you would enjoy this fact, in fact, I think it would make you jealous; would drive you crazy with jealousy; would eat you up inside like the fire eating your corpse: I have another boyfriend. No, Mother, I am not cheating: we are polyamorous.

Mother, I love him. I love him so much it could eat me up inside, outside, sideways; it could engulf me like the fire did your corpse: except: I would come out alive.

We met at a party. *Years ago*. But we re-met at a party last summer, sweating out our pores, leaking from all our orifices, our crevices crusted in sweat and want. That day they found out that my relationship was o p e n and so they o p e n e d me up and we fucked so good I thought I was dreaming (and maybe it's just because we were drunk, but the euphoria felt like it could cut me open and eat me from inside).

And then we fell in love, Mother.

We fell so in love that we could not untangle our knotted bodies.

I AM MY MOTHER'S DISAPPOINTMENTS

Our limp ball of yarn waited and caught another hopeless victim.

When I think of him it's like we're fucking for the first time all over again: it is like I am soaking with sweat and cum and alcohol: it is like he just found out he could fuck me and so he slithered inside me and couldn't find his way out.

You would love him, Mother. You would love him just as much as you love the other boy.

You would be so proud of me filling my life with love.

But then again, Mother, you might be so jealous of my freedom, of my communication, of my commitment to two people, that you hate me all over again. You might hate me with the sweet, patient hate that only a mother could give her child.

But I am still waiting for your blessing regardless. You can find me at home, in my dreams, waiting on the couch in the lobby of the dreamscape, legs crossed, fingers crossed, mind crossed, that you will come and tell me to continue being happy.

Cut

I would cut myself open if you would be able to bleed out of me. If acting like I was sixteen brought you back then I would cut every day. Please come back and yell at me. Please come back and wake me up. Sing me your lullabies. Bring me to the doctor for a broken toe. Make us open presents early because it's 2012 again and the world is ending. Stop my writing career now, throw it in the trash, come back and hold me like I am still a baby. If I could close my eyes and have you hold my hand again, rub my back as I fall asleep, turn on the lights to send me off to school, come home to baked goods, call you to cry about how sad I am that you killed yourself. If I could close my eyes and open them, I wish you would know that I'm looking for you.

I'm collecting mothers like flowers in a basket. Trying to fill myself to the brim with maternity and home baked sweets, trying to fill myself enough that I can forget you wanted to leave. I'm collecting mothers and I can't let them go, I can't let them abandon me again.

I wish there was a goal in mind, an amount of mothers that would fill the hole you left behind. I wish families could crowd together inside my broken heart and stitch me up. In less than a month you will kill yourself, ten years in the past. In less than a month I will be abandoned again and again and again, every year for ten years, in less than a month.

There won't be any mothers sending me flowers in a basket. It will just be me closing my eyes.

The Things

The thing about my grandmother is that she is still a feral teenager. She is all hate and angst and forgetfulness. She was never love and feathers and dust. She fell from the womb covered in sores, covered in tears, covered in thoughts about how much she's missed already and she is just missing more and more and more.

The thing about my grandmother is I forget I have her. I forget that she exists somewhere in this world with me. I only remember her in memories, mainly memories my mother told me, mainly memories of mean, ungrateful children, those memories are about my mother, those memories still hurt her.

The thing about my grandmother is she only seems to be in her mind sixteen percent of the time. I don't know where she lingers the rest of the time. Maybe she visits her children she likes, maybe she visits the grandchildren that bother to call, maybe she is off ranking the people in her life so she can choose the ones to beat.

I AM MY MOTHER'S DISAPPOINTMENTS

The thing about my grandmother is she was only a pity invite — who has a wedding and doesn't invite their grandmother? The person who made the person who made me. One side will be there (my dad's), one side will be watching (my mom's): grandfather already dead, grandmother somehow alive (do we still count her as alive?).

The thing about my mother is she never forgot it. She never forgot anything. She was like a machine. A lie detector, a copy machine, a hard drive with a shit ton of memory.

The thing about my mother is she never wanted anyone there, she was so lost in her shell that her mother welded to her that she almost always got spun around. She never knew if she was alive or dead. She seemed to forget — hiding in her blankets until she could tell if people could see her. My grandmother knew, she always knew. For her least favorite child, she kept notes and time stamps of all the things my mother could have been better at. It seemed like a scorecard, like if only my mother could make it to ten then she would have enough points to be a real daughter.

The thing about me is that I don't care until I do. I spent the night of my wedding happy and carefree. I prioritized the people closest to me. I never got a picture with my grandmother. I did get pictures with my dad's parents. I did get pictures with my parent. It is weird to hate the thing that brought your mother into the world. How much hate can you have for the thing that created her — my light, my master, my mother — how much can I hate that they all brought me into the world (there I was sitting inside my grandmother's uterus, waiting to get out).

The thing about the women in my family is that they are all so beautiful. So beautiful until they die and shrivel up like raisins, shrivel up like melting plastic under hot grease, shrivel up like a body in a flame. The women in my family are stunning until they lose their minds and then they are mannequins in corners, nobody is sure who moved them there.

please don't leaf us

thnx for the memories

I wish I could understand
the way that your mind was working.

Because I think back to some of the things you told me and I am left
mouth agape, staring.

I am editing this book that contains so much of you and me,
but there are still things I find myself afraid to discuss.

Do you remember the time that we were watching a
documentary together about the mother and daughter who were
doing porn together and you looked at me (maybe fifteen) and
said that when I was old enough we could do that and it would
make us so much money and if it's just for the money then there

I AM MY MOTHER'S DISAPPOINTMENTS

isn't anything actually weird or sexual about it *just like this mother and daughter said.*

Do you remember the time we were watching that documentary together about the girl who sold her virginity to pay for college and you told me to save mine up so I could sell it and pay for my own future and never take out loans.

Do you remember the time we were watching that documentary together about the guy who was bulimic and you cried that I was killing myself but I said that's not possible because I am anorexic.

I remember them. I think about them.

I think about your lack of focus on my specific ailments.

I think about your want to sexualize me but only for monetary gain.

Do you remember the time you got me and Sister thongs for Christmas, but I got girl-y froggy thongs because those aren't actually sexy and you gave my younger sister the woman-y lacey thongs because she didn't want to fuck.

Sex was always talked about in our house and often it was very positive and encouraging of who we wanted to be.

until it came to me.

Do you remember in your youth the times you were molested and raped, growing up in the system and trying to protect your younger sisters so you threw big fits to take some of the touch away from them.

In this memory I am reminded of you and the selflessness you exhibited.

But it leads me to the wonder of why you would want me to fill these shoes in anyway
anyway whatsoever. Why my body was always up for discussion. Do you remember.

Because I remember the way I felt my sexuality has to be monetized for it to be okay.

I AM MY MOTHER'S DISAPPOINTMENTS

Because I remember the way I felt when you told me
one day we could be porn stars together.
Because I remember being so confused by this because
I just wasn't interested.

But I didn't want to disappoint you back then so I watched the documentaries and I told you I'd think about it about anything about everything.

But I want to disappoint you now.

I only fuck for free.

The Gossip

Here is the 411, Mother: your husband probably fucked your best friend and yes she was still married to the man you at least pretended to like though nobody really knows if you did.

Here is the backstory, Mom: you left your husband, you killed yourself and he fell apart (let's be honest, we all knew he'd be useless without you), he was like jelly in the sun, he melted into her who was torn and broken and longing (it was always you, Mother, she was destined to fall in love with you Mother, she was always in love with you and the way you acted and the way people wanted you, she wanted you Mom, but she settled for Dad).

Here is how it went down, Mama: your loud mouth sister (you know the one) was speaking too loudly at prom and burst everyone's bubbles, *did you hear about J and B, did you hear that J and B have been together, did you hear they may have done some mouth stuff some hand stuff some sexual stuff, did you know did you know did you know*

Here is the aftermath, Mommy: there were parts of us that

thought maybe this is what happens now that maybe we conjoin families that were already conjoined but now we make it legal and now we are all siblings (even the ones who maybe wanna fuck) and now we can all be happy missing a parent, but that is not what happened — instead everyone just gained a bunch of resentment for each other and we lost and lost and fell apart so quickly it hurt.

I'm sorry, I know you're probably tired of hearing about it

but I have such a guilty conscience

—

are you waiting for me?

when was the last time you knew I would disappoint you?

is that what ended it all?

—

maybe it was supposed to be an escape,
you go, I go, we go, we hide

sometimes I write you notes in secret, I hide them with me
and I think of you
I think everything I do is because of you
everything, my failures
too

how can I celebrate Halloween without you?
(there are so many movies you would love)

I kill mothers in books just to avoid talking about you,

but then isn't that talking about you anyway?

How to cure obsession?

How to let my blood?

How to drain it all?

Learning to Forget

I went to school and went to school again and then I went to school

I remember you talking with Brother about the things he *should* be doing
    (of course he didn't do them; he's like you —
    programmed not to listen)

They must have slipped inside of me at night, because
I fear I took them to be my own

You *should* go to school (I did)
You *should* move out (I did)
You *should* listen to me (I'm trying)

                              You died too young,
                      You died when I was too young
                                to get my own list

                                      I'm improvising

I'll go back to school forever, I'll read books and books and books to try to make you proud, to try to get you out of my brain, to try to replace memories that hurt with fiction that heals, I will go back to school until you resurrect (you are my Jesus, you are my savior, you are the holy trinity and I will go into a desert or to a mall or into a cave if that means I will find you standing there), I'll go back to school, but if you could just answer me to let me know if that's what you want; I will go back to school until you show up to say you're proud of me or until I forget I ever had a mother.

I am the killer

Everyone dies, but maybe
I am the killer

Everyone dies, but
usually not so young

Everyone dies, but there should be
years without death, years without disease, years without mourning

I am the killer,
I murder my family to fuel myself.

I am the killer,
I want to write, I need the material, I need something to be sad about

So what if
I am the killer?

I know there are cancers and addictions and mental healths to blame,
but that all must start from somewhere (me, perhaps)

I am the killer,
sending my dreams into the world (I want to be a writer) and the world answers (so your family must die)

If only I would stop wanting,
I should stop being so selfish.

If I give up on my hopes and dreams,
will you come back Mom?

one day your mom will die too

Your mom is going to die. If she hasn't already, that is.

One day — your mom is going to be dead. One day — I won't be the girl with a dead mom. One day — we will all be girls with dead moms.

And what will I write about then, Mom? When I turn 33 and I've lived more than half of my life without you, what will I write about? When I outlive you and turn 39, what will I write about? When I am eighty and everyone's mom is dead, what will I write about? When will I outgrow the *dead mom* portion of my life? my career? my being? Who am I without the unique sadness of my dead mother? (this book would be nothing)

When your mother dies I hope I am around to hold you. I would like to pick up your hand, kiss your fingertips. I would like to make you spaghetti once a month for a year. I would like to make a nest of chewed debris that you can rest your head in.

How long do I have to be an orphan? Have I already aged out of it? My dad is still alive, he is so determined to make it to see

Halley's Comet but he has worked twenty seven days in a row, mostly sixteen hour days, so who knows if his body will allow it. If he dies before I reach your final age do you think it would count?

One day — you will have no parents. One day — I will have no parents. One day — I will have no one.

mother

i am editing this manuscript and i find myself more able than ever to process so much

> *i feel so much guilt all the time but through this manuscript*
> *i am able to understand:*
> *not all of the guilt i feel is my own*

mother

this manuscript was picked up once before but the press went under before it was released

i see now that this was meant to make noise, to make Girl Noise

past! present!

The normalcy of childhood is inherent to the child
to the parents   to the people   in the life of
the   child.

And you grow up and you realize that nobody is raised the same, or treated the same, or given the same as exactly everyone else   as exactly anyone else.

But I didn't realize my normal was crazed until now.

Now   I think about the ways in which my childhood is filled with mothering Mother and fathering Father, both of whom had lost their marbles. Likely, they never had any marbles to begin with. Likely, they had found lost marbles on the street and tried to make them their own. Likely, they were sharing three marbles   at most.

Now   I live with two people, two partners, two humans made of love, and I wonder how it has always felt normal. Has always been my normal. I never really had to question it.

I AM MY MOTHER'S DISAPPOINTMENTS

Now   I know this is because the normalcy of my childhood is *doing what feels right* and maybe thinking about it later, *doing what feels right* is just about all we had.

But back then   you were two teen kids in love, entering your twenties together with one baby already in tow. Back then you were two kids who just knew they had each other because let's be honest, all of the parents involved were trying their best and *doing what feels right*, but in a family of mental illness and addiction perhaps *what feels right* should be reconsidered, remanufactured, rebuilt but remembered.

But back then   you were trying your best. Now   early twenties with three kids. Both of you working as much as you can because the economy is never great for the poor. The kids are happy, they are smiling, they are all so unique and perfect. Now   we are kids being babysat by our aunt and wow Daddy is home! goodbye Aunt! thanks for watching us! But now there is a stranger at the do — there is MICHAEL MYERS at the door! — there is a killer inside the house and we run run RUN run! — Sister will fall to the ground screaming because there is a KILLER in our home and the adults are barely doing anything! so run run — I hide under the bed, curled into a corner, I feel the KILLER sit on the bed, holding Sister! — I silent-cry my silent tears, because I will miss Sister so much — but — it is Mom! the KILLER is my MOTHER and she isn't killing! it! was! just! a! joke!

Now   I do nightly checks with one of my partners to make sure the doors are locked and the house is locked and we are all locked up safe! Now   my other partner comes home, the partner who grew up in a gingerbread house with food always provided and no no no poor people. Now   I must do my check again. Now   danger may have leaked in. It is hard to remember to lock up your house when you are only used to sweetness entering.

Now   I question everything except for my own decisions. Which is to say, I question every movement I make and make no decisions. I have decided to love multiple people except this was never a decision, this is just how I experience the world. I am so bubbled up with love! So I spill spill spill into my partners. Normalcy.

But back then   I can remember Mommy and Daddy fighting over cigarettes again. I wish Mommy just wouldn't quit, would just accept this addiction so Daddy could come home and spend time and not have a knife pulled on him for just *listening* and *trying his best*.

But back then   violence is so normalized. Like Daddy and Brother trying to see who can hurt the other one the most. Like Mommy calling the cops on Daddy and Brother *again* because rough housing and violence are different and I think Daddy may have blacked out.

But back then   the cops would come sometimes. Didn't everyone have the cops come sometimes? Normalcy in calling the cops which is strange for two punks who hate the fucking pigs. But more than that there is normalcy in loving each other so much it hurts. And sometimes love is tough and sometimes we need to mediate our love, we need to learn what love feels like.

NOW   there is love in the house!

Brother is home with his children and his wife and oh my gosh they are so beautiful!

I AM MY MOTHER'S DISAPPOINTMENTS

Sister is with her boyfriend and cat and oh my gosh they are so beautiful!

Dad is away in another state with a woman who disowned us!

I am down the street with my two partners and our cat and oh my gosh they are so beautiful!

Now   I visit Brother with Sister and all our families are together. We talk about how we met Michael Myers and oh my gosh, *do you remember when Sister fell?* It was hilarious how we thought she was going to die! We all agree we must do this again, to our children, to our niblings, to the kids we bring into these houses. My partners look at each other. My partners' hive mind. My partners have agreed this is "one of those stories." But   we don't want kids anyway.

Then   we are just kids moving between Pennsylvania and North Carolina. We are just kids. We are just making the best out of life. We are running outside and playing in wet mud, wet sprinkles, soaking up the sun, we are all smiling SO! BIG!

Now   we are just kids who ask each other for help. We are just kids looking to help support each other. Brother and/or Sister is having a bad day? Should I send them some money to get a coffee? They do the same for me. We never stop spoon feeding each other love.

Then   Sister is spying on us and Mommy is paying her.

Then   Brother is in therapy for his anger issues.

Then   I am writing my silly little stories.

Now   I am writing my silly little stories. And also my

truths. Like this one. Though aren't they always baked in?
Now   I am taking a trauma dump on all of the pages of all of the books that I can. I am selling books about keeping my dead mother up at night. I am forever mourning the death of a woman I cannot know. I am hearing stories about your affairs. I am absorbing the ways in which we will always be tied together. I am lost in the past, feasting on nostalgia. I am sitting on my porch thinking about the happy memories. and. never. the. sad. ones.

How many   has nostalgia killed?

How long   will nostalgia be in jail for?

How often   can I visit nostalgia?

Then   I am growing up and everyone is dying. They are all jumping from buildings, or swallowing guns, or taking too many [drugs]. Everyone in my family always seems to be taking too many [drugs]. But some are prescribed! But some are not! But if you ask them, they will say don't worry! And I am a child! I want to not worry, but! I am at the funeral home again! I am being poked very hard by my aunt who has not yet killed herself, she is poking me because the love of her life just killed himself, but she is still together (for now); for now   she is not a broken body on the floor, she is a whole body poking me really hard and now I will be quiet. (sometime in the future i will learn this lesson, i will be quiet at her funeral and no one will poke me to remind me. i have learned by now, enough funerals have passed, i am quiet for you.)

Now   I am losing momentum, I hope you can't notice. I just want to tell you everything. I just want to split myself open for my insides to be on display. I want you to read me like a book. I will answer all the questions. To be honest, I am always ready to fill the hole. I am always ready to leak. I am always open to more love. I want to love myself full. I want to love myself. But I also just love you so so so so much, I wish I could kiss you right here. right now.

Now   the trauma dump is so ripe. Then   I am young and in love with every sentence people muster. I want to be cool and hang out with the cool   kids. the older   kids. Then   they are locking me in storage units and telling me I will be shot. Then   they are locking me in bathrooms with the lights forced off, they are chanting something to come and get me. Then   they are telling scary stories at sleepovers and they won't let me leave, they tell me they are out there waiting, they are making it so so dark. Now   I sleep with nightlights all over the place. Now   I write the scary stories.

Then   I don't know where Mommy is. I am searching around and around for her in all the cracks and crevices but! There she is! She is in the hospital, she is taking care of herself. We are visiting, all of the kids and her husband. Daddy kisses her head like that could cure her.

Then   Mommy is dying. Mommy is always dying. She is falling asleep in the shower in the tub in any water that she might be able to finally drown in. She is choking in the house alone while we are at the pool — Gramps finds her and saves her. She is breaking into hives ~~at stress~~ at a spider biting her vagina that she has no feeling in, back broken from a disease she cannot control. She is slipping into her pills. She is slipping into sleep. Mommy will die young, I am always shocked she did not die   younger.

Now

     Then

         Always

        I am spiraling into
        spaghetti bowl thoughts
        as my insides noodle and
        explode.
    Always

         roaming and roasting
        and churning the past
        and future and
        the smell of the present.
    Always

         living in any time but the
now.

Now their hands hold me. Now I can close my sleepy eyes. Now I am so filled up with love.

Warning Signs

My body is falling apart, Mom. And I'm prepared to blame you.

You gave me the warnings: do not be a waitress, do not strip, do not have three children, do not inherit the genetics of our family. I have never become a stripper (though if I had any rhythm at all I would have wanted to try), I do not want children (at least, especially, right now), and I was only a bartender. By definition I have only done one.

Mom, I can think back to the time you found out that I cut myself. You and me at the doctors for an annual and they ask me to roll up my sleeve to take my pulse. Your eyes, your eyes. I can picture your voice now telling me: *you can't do that, they're going to blame me and take you away*. I can remember my own thoughts: all you care about is yourself.

It is not easy to mourn you. The first few years were nothing but happy memories flooding my ears, flooding my brain. My friends telling me about how much they missed you. We were the house everyone came to. We didn't even have money or accommodations or anything, really (we weren't even a house but a small apartment that sat underground). We had love and love and love and understanding. Friends would fill our house for Sunday dinners. We would fit over ten people in our home and you would cook and plate and ask everyone how their days were. And you actually listened. You asked them to explain all their worries and you listened. My friend Ashira came over just to talk to you, she came to you because you were a home that people love.

But it was hard to live there with nowhere else to go. There was so much love in our home, but so so much violence. I think you and Dad were used to growing up in mosh pits and using your bodies to protect yourself so you were prepared to take a beating from your kids or give a beating to your kids. I remember you and Brother fighting everywhere. Your bad back, misaligned, genetically inadequate, tousled around and you would fight back and you would wrestle and you would scream and cry and then you wouldn't be able to walk for days. I remember your back breaking and you warning us that it is genetic and it is coming for us. I remember Brother always got the worst of it. I remember you smacking me when I tried to stand up for Sister. I remember you telling your mother you wouldn't hit us with a hairbrush. I remember you kicking Brother out of the car for not liking the Beatles.

But I don't fight like you did. Not anymore. My body is nothing but sensitivity now. I used to love cutting myself open and watching all of my insides move around, but now my muscles cramp and crust and I'm in pain for days because my anxiety, my depression, my ADHD, my everything bleeds into my body so much that my body tenses and loses all ability to be fluid. I spend days feeling every movement in my body and I do the physical therapy I learned and I put on a brave face. But my body wants to hurt me. My partner told me my body got used to physical pain as a way to process emotion. I started self-harming in eighth grade and I didn't stop until I was well into my undergraduate degree. I still think about it. My addictive personality craves it. I've learned no real coping mechanisms. I've learned no fruitful grieving techniques. Sometimes I feel like I've learned nothing.

But my partners massage out the kinks. They will rub my ailing body because they know that I don't know how. They use their soft, perfect hands to try to rub out the sadness that boils under my skin.

But I still don't know how to grieve you.

I find you in everything. I feel you in my body.

You told me one day my back, too, will crack under the pressure of carrying your genetics. So I try to stay in academia where I don't have to bend and grab and run around, but the pay is shit and I have no insurance. I try to baby my body into feeling like it can relax, but I've had arthritis in both of my knees since I was fourteen. I don't think I know how to relax. I keep telling myself that one day I will know how.

But you never did. You worked and worked and worked until your back deteriorated so much that you were mostly bedridden. I try to talk to my siblings now but all of our memories are different. Brother seems to see with a golden hue and I think this may be from guilt. None of us were great to each other, but all of us were so so happy to be family and we had so much love. Brother, I do not blame you, but I must be honest: we had a dysfunctional childhood. It's not your fault, it's not our fault. Honestly, I think it was mostly fueled by a mother who didn't know how to unhinge herself from her emotions to put us first. She watched her best friend fuck up her children through so many lies that she didn't realize her unnecessary honesty could do the same. But we can all be fucked up for different reasons. Sister has lost the memories of you. She remembers you through us and through pictures and videos, but you killed yourself with two of your children home and neither of them can live it down.

I don't know how to mourn you, Mom. Because now when I think back to you I think of the ways in which I would still be stuck in PA if you were alive. I'd probably still be dating one of my abusive exes. I would never have written the books that I have. My life wouldn't look like what it is now and I am so so happy with where it is going.

Does that make me happy you're dead? Everytime my back hurts I miss you. Everytime I see photos of you I wish I could tell you all of the things I'm doing now. But these things only exist because you aren't here.

I miss you so much, Mom and I hope you read my other books and find the happiness I had in my childhood and with you, I hope you find the pain of mourning a wonderful mother, I hope you understand that I am not the same without you.

I miss you so much, Mom but I hope you read this book and understand that I am not the same without you; I have grown up and realized that I did not like everything you did and just because someone is dead does not mean they were perfect, I hope you understand that I'm just as disappointed with you as you are with me. I hope you understand how much I love you.

You'd Be So Happy

Brother is doing well with his babies (one on the way and Daughter who is thriving). You'd love his fiance (who is basically his wife). Sister-in-law is spooky, she is a horror girl, she is also loud, she would stand up to you, she would take Brother's side when he is right and yours when he is wrong. Brother and Sister-in-law are good parents, you would be so proud. Niece is nice, but she can also kick, she can also headbutt, she can also give someone a bloody nose if she wants to. Nephew is still cooking, but I know he will be great.

Sister is doing well with her life. She is about to graduate with a degree in children, she will graduate and know so much about babies and one day she might have a baby. You would be so proud of her brain and her energy. She will never let someone walk all over her and that might bring you to tears. She is strong and independent and she is the funniest person I have ever met.

Brother and Sister are doing so many good things in life it makes me well up with pride, well up with happiness, I am bloated with love for them.

But I Do Not Know About Dad

Let me start with: he loves us. That would never change, could never change, he would never stop loving his children if his life depended on it.

But he did leave us. He followed a woman (let's call her Cunt) to another state in a different time zone and he left Brother and Sister and Grandchildren. Dad has become a dad, a bit more absentee, a bit more dislocated, he has fallen off the road and into a stream.

I could have gotten behind it if it wasn't for the way in which Cunt left and dad followed. I could have understood the decision if Cunt didn't write a letter blaming all us Siblings, if maybe she had talked this out like an adult, if maybe I didn't write her all those recommendation letters just so she could tell dad it was actually me to blame, it was Sister's fault, don't leave Brother out of it.

Cunt couldn't get over you. She never met you, but she knew how much we loved you, she knew how much we missed you, she knew what you meant to us. *Aren't you over it yet*, she'd ask us, but we all know there is no answer that could suffice.

She was obsessed with you, Mother. Even in your death you seem to possess people, you seem to swallow them whole until they die slowly inside of you. She didn't want to be our mother, she just wanted us to forget we ever had one.

And so she left, she wrote goodbye to us all, she moved out of the house that Sister was sitting in — *just redecorating*.

She goes, he goes. The pact we never knew about.

mom and me

Acknowledgments

Thank you, Diana. The love and care you put into this book fills me with so much joy. This book is so special to me and it means the world that we were able to bring it into the world together. I appreciate you, your energy, your mission, and your writing. Thank you.

Thank you to my partners for reading these stories and inspiring me to write these stories. I could not put myself out there without you to hold me.

Thank you, Sister, for the way you carry me in your heart and for the way you allow me to carry you. I find you in everything.

Thank you, Brother, for the insight and knowledge you bring to this world. I can't imagine the world spinning without you there to mock it.

Thank you, Dad, for reading this book more than once. For creating a space where we can be critical and retrospective. For your unconditional love.

Thank you to my friends and family who read this book in earlier stages. Thank you Andy, Morghen, Greg, Hollie, Lydia, Amber, Kate, Kaitlyn, Katlyn, Sarah(s), Krislyn, and all the people who inspire my writing and vulnerability.

Thank you, Mom.

About the Author

Victoria holds an MA in English from the University of Maine. Originally from Pennsylvania, she now resides in Maine with her partners and elderly cat while teaching at her alma mater. She is the author of a collection of short stories *My Haunted Home* (FC2) and chapbooks *Death and Darlings* and *Entries of Boredom and Fear* (Bottlecap Press). Overall, she hopes to discomfort, humor and charm.